Midlife Crisis Cars

MATT MASTER

BBC
BOOKS

CONTENTS

3

INTRODUCTION
ORIGIN OF THE SPECIES

Ever since early man gazed into a muddy puddle and noticed with monosyllabic alarm an extra degree of grizzle to his simian features, or observed the relative ease with which younger hunter-gatherers slotted into their sabre-toothed loin cloths, there has existed the Midlife Crisis.

The emotional evolution of the gut-sucking, toupee-wearing skirt-chaser is distinctly limited. Only the means by which the change manifests itself has altered with time: a sharper spear, a darker cave, a broader sword, a bigger codpiece. Cometh the 20th century, cometh the car, and with it the most direct and visceral means of denying one's mortality and the terror of middle-age spread.

Lean, fast, powerful – the sports car offers up the very essence of youth, but it's also expensive and therefore denied the young in favour of those with accumulated wealth; the only kickback from getting fat and realizing not even your wife fancies you any more. There is, of course, a sliding scale of midlife crisis severity, known in psychiatric circles as the Follicle Formula. As one eminent Belgian practitioner once said: 'The greater the pate, the more certain his fate,' as helpfully illustrated in our key below.

0 DIGNITY INTACT

1 WORRYING THE WIFE

2 FOOLING NU-ONE

3 EMBARRASSING THE KIDS

4 LAUGHED AT BY STRANGERS

5 SPORTS JACKET TO STRAIGHT JACKET

The following pages provide a highly scientific analysis of the varied and complex unions of magnificent machine and misguided man. Part celebration, part condemnation, all of it uncomfortable, irrefutable truth. Buckle up, Baldy.

ONE
THE
MESSY
DIVORCE

FERRARI MONDIAL CABRIOLET

9

PRODUCTION: 1980–92
0–60MPH: 8 seconds
TOP SPEED: 143mph
CRISIS RATING: 4

There are few men who have not, at some point in their lives, desired to own a Ferrari. There are fewer still who ever find both financial and family commitments abate in time to turn dream into reality. But when the missus has packed the kids into your smoky Volvo and headed off to her mum's for the foreseeable, well, time's a-wasting, chum.

The Mondial was, and still is, Ferrari's only 'entry-level' car. Underpowered and understyled, it still sold almost 7,000 units in its 12-year run. Big numbers for a yesteryear Italian sports car.

The mid-mounting of a V8 engine allowed for decent rear seats, the ideal balance of proper handling and space for weekend visitation rights. The cabriolet first appeared in 1983, upping the price and lowering the structural rigidity. Performance was lacklustre compared to cars a quarter of its price, and with the iconic Testarossa and F40 being sold alongside it, this was effeminacy personified in Ferrari form.

Few cars smack harder of desperation than the Mondial: a Ferrari for those who can't afford one; a sports car for those who don't like performance; a two-seater for those who still need four seats. But, boy, could it piss off the wife.

PORSCHE 914

PRODUCTION: 1969–76
0–60MPH: 13 seconds
TOP SPEED: 118mph
CRISIS RATING: 1

The struggle to make sports cars profitable has produced a variety of dubious projects, one of the most bum-clenchingly embarrassing being the 914, a joint venture between performance purist Porsche and shopping trolley specialist Volkswagen.

The wildly ambitious outcome was two visually identical cars, but one with a Beetle engine to be sold as a Volkswagen, and one with a proper flat-six to be sold as a Porsche. (Bear in mind that this was the 1960s and even the suits in Wolfsburg were probably passing something rather stronger than Old Holborn round the boardroom table).

Mercifully someone at Porsche put the bong down for long enough to twig that this was commercial suicide for both parties, and the car was badged up as a Porker regardless of what lay beneath.

It sold slowly and mostly to Californians, eventually being replaced by the emphatically more modern 924. Production balls-ups meant it ended up costing almost as much as a 911, all the while being tarred with the VW brush, making anyone who bought one look both a bit tight and a bit stupid.

MGB **ROADSTER**

13

PRODUCTION: 1962–80
0–60MPH: 11 seconds
TOP SPEED: 105mph
CRISIS RATING: 1

The social liberation that defined the 1960s took many forms. People smoked weed, dropped acid, banged drums, tambourines, your wife, whatever they could lay their hands on. The grey area created by free love brought plenty of business to the divorce courts, and almost as much to dealerships flogging the MGB Roadster. After all, what greater cure for cuckoldry could there be than the long overdue ownership of that pretty little British sports car you always wanted but could never afford while the wife was buying kaftans and giving suspiciously large tips to the milkman?

A car more wholeheartedly embodying the very essence of free-spirited motoring it is hard to imagine. The MGB was cheap, attractive and quintessentially English. It was also slow, noisy and liable to rust at the slightest provocation, but none of this even registered with a generation of baby-boomers who'd grown up on condensed milk and Ford Anglias. Escapist stuff then as it is today, although the mandatory garb of cloth cap and string-back gloves must now be accompanied by a massive beard, membership of CAMRA and no social skills.

BMW M3 CONVERTIBLE

PRODUCTION: 1988–91
0–60MPH: 6.5 seconds
TOP SPEED: 146mph
CRISIS RATING: 2

The combination of speed and exposure to the elements is a vital one, despite the dangers imposed upon fragile comb-overs and easily sun-burnt scalps. When BMW went racing in Germany's touring car series they built an iconic small sports car in the homologated E30 M3. Putting competition underpinnings into a road car created a twitchy but inspirational legend. Chopping the roof off so they could sell it to men more focused on the clipped 'tache than the clipped apex did it very few favours.

Around 18,000 original M3s were made, and mercifully just 786 faced the angle grinder. That said, with between 200 and 215bhp on tap from a shortened version of the straight six from BMW's M1 supercar, this was the world's fastest four-seat convertible throughout the late 1980s and early 1990s. Nowadays the coupé commands mega money and is edging its way from track-day trophy to collectors' item. The cabriolet still just makes you look like a pimp.

CONTE AMPHIBIOUS CAR

PRODUCTION: What? Sorry, was miles away
0–60MPH: Can't remember
TOP SPEED: Look, that's missing the point
CRISIS RATING: 3

Not every divorcee is seeking approval from the nearest blonde. Nor is speed necessarily the only means of encouraging the kids out for a Sunday drive when they are being maliciously spoiled by their mother. The discerning few curried favour with the fruits of their loins by 'investing' in the Conte amphibious car. What child could resist the prospect of ploughing straight on when lesser dads would be forced to park up or drown?

This was truly the only means of travel for the emancipated man, and surely the soundest assertion to any detractors that alimony and dinners for one have not dampened that adventurous spirit. (Disregard the wistful shoreward glance of the boy in the back. He's not afraid, he's probably just forgotten something).

LOTUS **ECLAT**

PRODUCTION: 1974–82
0–60MPH: 7.8 seconds
TOP SPEED: 129mph
CRISIS RATING: 2

Hidden amidst the impenetrable wilds of north Norfolk is one of our greatest automotive institutions. Lotus has been building plastic cars in a shed near Norwich for half a century, each one looking great, gripping like a pit bull grips your leg in early spring, and offering just one dependable trait: that they will break down in a truly ruinous fashion when you least expect it.

But that, as any British sports car enthusiast will tell you, is part of the charm. The Eclat was Lotus' first concerted attempt at making a genuinely practical car, using the Elite platform but designing a fastback-style rear end with big boot and, good God man, proper rear seats. Built in a period when supercars were swelling with more cylinders and more power, the Eclat never developed more than a modest 160bhp from its home-grown 2.2-litre engine, relying instead on light weight and superior handling to see off the competition.

So what you got in theory was the ultimate package for a patriotic family man with a small fetish for G-forces. In practice, you got very familiar with the hard shoulder, the RAC and innovative ways to entertain children with a spanner, a torch and a tartan blanket.

ALFA ROMEO **SPIDER**

PRODUCTION: 1966–93
0–60MPH: 11.3 seconds
TOP SPEED: 111mph
CRISIS RATING: 1

There are few greater associations between movie and motor than that of *The Graduate* and the Alfa Romeo Spider. Dustin Hoffman's liberation between Mrs Robinson's thighs and behind the Alfa's wheel speaks to the eternal adolescent in all of us. The Italian embodiment of escapism, opportunity and shameless 1960s sexuality, it's small wonder that us simple blokes have been turning to the Spider in a forlorn bid to recapture our fleeting youth for decades since. The catch is that even Dustin Hoffman looked ridiculous in a car only ever suited to pretty Tuscan signoras in gigantic sunglasses and tiny skirts.

All elegant Pininfarina curves and modest little engines, the Spider evolved for almost thirty years, each generation getting progressively less sporty and no more masculine than the last. A lovely little thing, then, but certain only to add new dimensions to a man's middle-aged self-doubt.

JENSEN HEALEY

PRODUCTION: 1972–6
0–60MPH: 7.8 seconds
TOP SPEED: 120mph
CRISIS RATING: 1

The relative obscurity of the Jensen Healey is attributable to a number of factors both within and beyond the control of its makers. The union in 1972 of two great British marques to make a small two-seat sports car seems like a recipe for success on paper. And you can't really blame them for not seeing the 1970s oil crisis coming. Even cannibalizing parts from period Austins and Vauxhalls is forgivable, but when it comes to sourcing an engine, it's hard to think of a company less advisable to turn to than Lotus, especially when the engine in question was entirely untested.

But in four years some 10,000 Jensen Healeys rolled off the West Bromwich factory line, spurting enough oil about the place to cause a fuel crisis all of its own, and rusting so readily that virtually none remain.

Strangely enough, though, this hopeless union of blindly ambitious British engineering, coupled with unpretentious styling and a James Dean-style early demise, makes the Jensen Healey rather cool today.

TWO
BOND,
PREMIUM
BOND

PORSCHE 911

PRODUCTION: 1964–present
0–60MPH: 8.3 seconds (at launch)
TOP SPEED: 130mph (at launch)
CRISIS RATING: 4

So you've come into a bit of cash. Football pools, premium bonds, pushing the mother-in-law down the stairs. And what better way to exploit your newfound riches than by blowing the lot on another car?

The default supercar for the post-war European male is, was, and probably always will be, the Porsche 911. Although finely honed and all too ordinary today, it was a unique proposition a few years back, both in terms of its appearance and its handling. Or rather, the lack thereof. Porsche ran a sort of accidental eugenics programme for the best part of thirty years, by producing a car that appealed to one of society's least likeable types, and then promptly wrapped him around a tree.

Launched in 1964 as a sporting replacement to the Beetle, with an air-cooled six-cylinder engine squashed into what ought to have been the boot, it was anathema to the point-and-squirt school of British sports car building. But for all its high-speed foibles, the 911 retained the respect of the motoring cognoscenti for its superior engineering and deft, albeit pregnable, agility. And despite its relative modesty in terms of cost and appearance, it remains the ultimate automotive symbol of Thatcherite greed and a face full of white powder.

LOTUS **ESPRIT**

PRODUCTION: 1976–2004
0–60MPH: 7.1 seconds (at launch)
TOP SPEED: 135mph (at launch)
CRISIS RATING: 1

It's a fact all too readily overlooked these days that one of the most inspired and ridiculous supercars of the 1970s and '80s actually came from Blighty. The mighty (and mighty fragile) Lotus Esprit was penned into a vicious wedge by Italian design house Giugiaro and built out of fibreglass, trees and cows by our own boys in Norfolk.

Sublime handling made up for typically inconsequential Lotus power, and the generous application of plastic meant low kerb-weight and things that actually wouldn't rust.

The fact that Roger Moore drove one up a beach in *The Spy Who Loved Me* did no harm to the Esprit's global recognition back in the days of velour and Asti Martini, and even today you can't help but gawp as one squeaks and pops its way past at knee level.

No one could resent you for buying a Lotus Esprit: it was British, it looked the business, and everyone knew it'd be knackered by this time next week anyway.

BUGATTI EB110

PRODUCTION: 1991–5
0–60MPH: 4.5 seconds
TOP SPEED: 219mph
CRISIS RATING: 4

Now that windfall needs to be large to afford an EB110; either that, or you have to be shagging a sheikh. Costing around £280,000 in 1991 and looking like nothing on earth, the EB110 was demonstrably the ultimate car for its brief production cycle. With a carbon fibre chassis built by an aircraft manufacturer, scissor doors and a 60 valve V12 with four (yes FOUR) turbo chargers, the final evolution of the EB110 topped out at 219mph and turned your internal organs to soup on the way there.

If you needed any more reassurance that you'd spent wisely (and let's face it, you might), one Michael Schumacher bought a banana yellow 590bhp Supersport version in 1994. Then the company went bust the following year, making the pair of you look like utter monkeys.

Only 139 EB110s are believed to have been made, so they still command silly money. But you can get four of them for the price of a Veyron, so they're technically a bargain.

ASTON MARTIN V8

PRODUCTION: 1969–90
0–60MPH: 5.4 seconds (at launch)
TOP SPEED: 162mph (at launch)
CRISIS RATING: 0

The last proper car that Aston Martin ever made was the simply-named V8. Proper because it was hand-built out of steel and walnut, trimmed in Connolly leather and kept well away from any of those nasty modern gimmicks like fuel injection or competent handling.

This afforded the V8 an unassailable level of class the likes of which modern Astons can only dream of. And it still does. Get onboard and it's like being given membership to your own private gentlemens' club. Fire the carburetted V8 upfront and you could feel the hairs sprouting on your chest with every lazy prod of throttle. Drive it hard and you seem to define the very British notion of point-and-squirt. Truly a sports car for a man's man, with none of those airy-fairy Italian cornering abilities.

Somehow the V8 remained Aston's principal product for over twenty years. More Bond connotations prolonged its anachronistic existence right up to 1990, at which point it all went south for Aston Martin and the English gent went elsewhere.

FERRARI TESTAROSSA

PRODUCTION: 1984–92
0-60MPH: 5.2 seconds
TOP SPEED: 179MPH
CRISIS RATING: 4

The 1980s remains the decade synonymous with excess, and no car better fits that brief than the Ferrari Testarossa. Fulfilling more adolescent fantasies than Kim Basinger ever did back then, this car truly was the poster boy for a period of shameless self-indulgence and absolutely massive hair. Coming in at a monstrous 6.5 feet wide and still managing to be well under 4 feet high, the Testarossa's appearance implied a speed so phenomenal that it had flattened itself against the road. A midships 390bhp boxer V12 made sure appearances weren't deceptive either, and gave it the soundtrack to match.

So exclusive was the Testarossa that when the producers of *Miami Vice* decided to include the now infamous white example in their TV series, they couldn't get hold of one and cobbled together a fairly amateurish replica. Ferrari was predictably apoplectic and promptly dispatched the real thing to replace it.

Few Ferraris, few sports cars for that matter, are as instantly recognizable as the Testarossa. A glorious union of form and function, it marked you out then, just as it does today, as an absolute tool. But a very, very lucky tool at that.

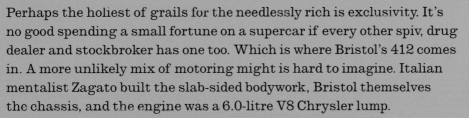

BRISTOL **412**

PRODUCTION: 1975–82
0–60MPH: 7.8 seconds
TOP SPEED: 140mph
CRISIS RATING: 4

Perhaps the holiest of grails for the needlessly rich is exclusivity. It's no good spending a small fortune on a supercar if every other spiv, drug dealer and stockbroker has one too. Which is where Bristol's 412 comes in. A more unlikely mix of motoring might is hard to imagine. Italian mentalist Zagato built the slab-sided bodywork, Bristol themselves the chassis, and the engine was a 6.0-litre V8 Chrysler lump.

The result was an impossibly pricey sort of convertible, sort of sportscar-cum-grand-tourer thing. Sort of. And you could be sure absolutely no one else had one, because absolutely no one else wanted one.

The principle drawback, aside from being styled like a house brick, was that it was so rare that no one knew what it was, and so anonymous that no one cared enough to ask.

DE TOMASO **PANTERA**

PRODUCTION: 1970–91
0–60MPH: 5.5 seconds
TOP SPEED: 129mph
CRISIS RATING: 3

Somehow or other the De Tomaso Pantera stayed in production for over twenty years, but individual models rarely stayed on the road for over twenty minutes. In fact a number of high-profile celebrities took their last corner in this car, whose principal safety feature appears to have been a 50/50 chance of starting. This particular problem entered automotive folklore when Elvis got so angry with the godawful reliability of his early Pantera that he got out his gun and shot it.

De Tomaso had borrowed a nigh on bomb-proof V8 from Ford, then had the inspired idea of mating it to the cheapest transmission it could lay its hands on. Fit and finish were also absolutely dreadful, and chronic rust was seemingly part of the standard equipment.

Rarity, Italian pedigree and stunning styling, however, papered over the cracks for De Tomaso, who sold over 7,000 of this model, the vast majority of which went to the ever-gullible US market.

We can only guess at how many an American mid-life crisis was quickly and often violently compounded by the purchase of a Pantera, probably in the shape of epic bills, gigantic accidents and the ever-nearing spectre of divorce.

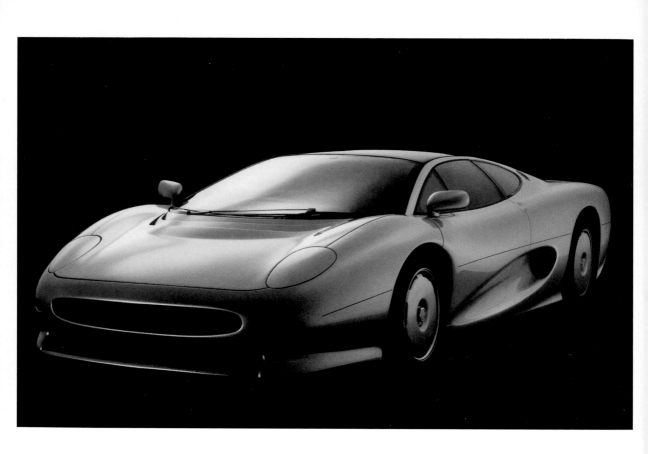

JAGUAR XJ220

PRODUCTION: 1992–4
0–60MPH: 4.0 seconds
TOP SPEED: 217mph
CRISIS RATING: 5

When you're in the throes of a midlife crisis, and about to drop a small fortune on a supercar to make it all better again, there are some things you just don't need to hear. Now imagine you've put a non-refundable £50,000 deposit down on a radical new £360,000 Jaguar that will have four-wheel drive, scissor doors and a massively high-performance V12 engine to rival the likes of Ferrari and Lamborghini. Bloody marvellous. It'll be the elixir of eternal youth. You'll be the envy of all your friends and fighting off blondes with gigantic boobs at every set of traffic lights. Surely? I mean, come on. What could possibly go wrong?

Wait three whole years and you get a phone call. Someone in a rather croaky voice is telling you something: 'Er, that car you're contractually obliged to buy. A few changes: it's got rear wheel drive, ordinary doors and an engine that's half the size and plagued by wicked turbo-lag. Oh, and the price has gone up by over £40,000. Sorry.' Clunk. Dial tone.

You are not thrilled. But Jaguar, being a big-hearted sort of an organization, offers you the chance to buy your way out of the contract. And to crown it all, the judge finds in Jaguar's favour when you attempt to sue. How's that crisis working out for you?

LAMBORGHINI **TRACTOR**

PRODUCTION: 1949–Present
0–60MPH: n/a
TOP SPEED: 30mph
CRISIS RATING: 4

Clothes, food, cars, girls: whatever rings your bell in life, there's always someone trying to convince you that Italian is a byword for the best. And the same, weirdly, goes for farming. In post-war Italy, Ferruccio Lamborghini began a tractor factory, assembling agricultural machines out of leftover bits of military hardware. It was the success of this business that funded his foray into supercars, and for some that's still just a sideline.

A Lambo tractor is to the udder-tugging fraternity what a Murciélago is to the investment banker. A piece of automated art, an indulgence, a sign that, whether you're wading through silage or stock options, you've made it.

THREE
SHOESTRING
FELLOWS

OPEL KADETT GT/E

PRODUCTION: 1975–9
0–60MPH: n/a
TOP SPEED: 118mph
CRISIS RATING: 3

Moments of grim middle-aged introspection are not the preserve of the mega-rich, but seeking out your second coming on a strict budget is a serious challenge. The Opel Kadett is the car that gave birth to the Vauxhall Astra, reason enough to run a mile, but in 1975 the Kadett GT/E was to West Germany what that Ford Mustang was to blue-collar America; a working man's triumph. Honest, simple, unpretentious and fast. Or fast-ish. A fuel injection 1.9-litre engine put out a modest 115bhp, but crucially it was fed through the skinny rear tyres alone, providing scope for hairy-chested handling heroics. Impossibly rare special editions have now attained cult status, most notably the Black Magic and, er, the Swinger. No hint of a crisis there, then.

PANTHER **KALLISTA**

PRODUCTION: 1982–90
0–60MPH: 8 seconds
TOP SPEED: No one dared
CRISIS RATING: 4

If you couldn't afford a classic British sports car back in the mid-1980s, you still had options. One was the bus, the other the Panther Kallista. Started in Surrey in 1972 and, perhaps tellingly, bust by 1980, Panther Westwinds was bought out by a Korean businessman determined to build sports cars but only capable of such automotive drivel as this.

Looking every inch the Asian misinterpretation of the Morgan that it was, the sinfully ugly and incompetent Kallista sold only to the sort of person able to convince himself that its rarity was indicative of his unique good taste, rather than utter imbecility or terrible eyesight. Offered with a four-speed manual or three-speed auto screwed to a four-cylinder Ford lump, the Kallista didn't go terribly well, and did even worse when it was stationary.

FORD CAPRI

PRODUCTION: 1969–86
0–60MPH: 8.6 seconds (at best)
TOP SPEED: 120mph (at best)
CRISIS RATING: 2

Most cars that are truly engraved on the British psyche are inextricably linked with cucumber sandwiches, cold showers and interfering with the help. Aston, Rolls, Bentley, you know the sort of thing. But there is one that endures as ably as any of these, says as much about being British, and yet can enter that hallowed pantheon without so much as wiping the dogshit off its boots: the Ford Capri.

A deliberate attempt by Ford of Europe to emulate the success of the Mustang in America, the Capri was always meant to be a working class hero, no-nonsense, affordable to all but still deeply desirable.

Ford flogged nearly two million Capris worldwide, and earned a cult following in the UK which still exists today. Synonymous with a more casual, insular, island era of drink-driving, unprotected sex and five-pint-fuelled fisticuffs, this was unshackled masculinity in motoring form, the likes of which we haven't seen since.

Various subtle evolutions over its 17-year lifespan never altered the basic, almost Freudian format of long bonnet, small cockpit and unsophisticated rear-wheel drive handling. This was the penis extension for those who definitely didn't need one. Definitely. Got it?

NISSAN 300ZX

PRODUCTION: 1984–9
0–60MPH: 6.7 seconds
TOP SPEED: 145mph
CRISIS RATING: 2

Perhaps the only thing that defines the 1980s more succinctly than rolling up the sleeves of your jacket and deserving to be punched in the jewels is the unutterable dross we called sports cars. Long gone were the days of hand-built, low-volume masterpieces, lovingly crafted by little old men with three generations of panel beating behind them and a roll-up stuck to their lip. By the time the Nissan 300ZX turned up a sports car was a mass-production item, unceremoniously spat off a sterile production line somewhere very foreign and served up to you with all the care and emotion of a Domino's pizza.

That the 300ZX was actually quite good, quick-ish with its 3.0-litre V6, agile on a half-decent chassis and even able to win at Le Mans one year doesn't detract from the fact that this was the TV dinner of the sports car world: cheap, unlovable, unimaginative, vacuum-packed.

An age-old problem with Japanese car design was the propensity to nick ideas steeped in cultural reference and brand lineage, cobble them all together and pray to God, or Buddha, that they came out looking like the real deal. So the 300ZX gets fastback styling, pop-up lights, a Targa roof, big V6, and still ends up looking, well, ordinary.

MARCOS MANTULA SPYDER

PRODUCTION: 1984–93
0–60MPH: 5.7 seconds
TOP SPEED: 154mph
CRISIS RATING: 3

If you really couldn't shell out on keeping the grey hairs hidden, only marginally more expensive than a bottle of Just For Men was the Marcos Mantula Spyder. The idea was you could buy a high-performance British sports car at half the cost by cutting out the middle man. By which Marcos meant they'd deliver it to you in bits.

The beauty of selling a car in kit form is that, if and when it goes horribly wrong, you can just blame the person who built it. And in the case of Marcos, who went into receivership twice a week, no one was ever going to be there to answer the phone anyway.

So it paid to be handy, both in and under your Marcos, for if it wasn't spitting you off the road, it was leaving you stranded at the side of it. A great British institution, all flat caps and derring-do in the 1960s, had by the mid-80s morphed into a poor man's TVR. And that's the equivalent of saying 'like Bernard Manning, but racist'.

PEUGEOT 504 COUPÉ

PRODUCTION: 1969–83
0–60MPH: 12.6 seconds
TOP SPEED: 107mph
CRISIS RATING: 4

The exact nature and severity of the problem facing middle-aged man is painfully highlighted by the bloke who goes out to buy something 'a bit sporty' and comes back with a family car that's had the rear doors welded shut. The Peugeot 504 was launched as an 82bhp saloon in 1968, with a seriously half-cocked coupé and convertible appearing the following year. If a further reminder was need as to just how unsporty the 504 was, 1970 saw the unveiling of an estate version and diesel engines being offered across the range.

Seldom has the bell of denial rung louder as embittered, chain-smoking Frenchmen tore about in these spongy two-doors, their nauseated kids crammed into the foreshortened rear while the missus planned her next infidelity from the passenger seat.

Then, to add insult to self-inflicted injury, Peugeot actually started making a 504 pick-up, and the fate of the coupé was complete.

RELIANT SCIMITAR GTE

PRODUCTION: 1968–75
0–60MPH: 9.3 seconds
TOP SPEED: 126mph
CRISIS RATING: 1

Dubbing it the world's first ever sporting estate car, Reliant was hoping to invent an uncontested niche with the Scimitar GTE. And why not? The mid-'70s was a time of radical invention, of embracing new things, of failing to realize quite what all that LSD had actually gone and done.

But it still wouldn't have taken a member of Mensa to point out to the powers that be that their car was really just an impractical estate and rubbishy, daft-looking sports car thrown haphazardly together, like the lovechild of an unfortunate union between someone really mumsy and a sleazy double-glazing salesman.

A second glance at Reliant's own catalogue picture says it all. Long gone are the days when Health and Safety or advertising standards would turn a blind eye to that little girl and her impending trip to the orthodontist.

Still, it had a V6 engine and a big boot, thereby providing countless despairing dads with a last glimmer of hope. Here, perhaps, was all the car they'd ever need. Practicality and performance, and it looks like a bargain to boot! It almost seems cruel, looking back on it…

OPEL **MANTA**

PRODUCTION: 1975–81
0–60MPH: 11 seconds
TOP SPEED: 109mph
CRISIS RATING: 2

63

The Manta was another one of those working men's motors. The sort of thing you loved your dad for owning when you were small enough to be shoehorned into the back, only to realize on reaching adolescence that it was a deeply embarrassing pile of crap and spanners that seemingly only you and he had ever bought into.

But not to worry, because for those halcyon days when the sun was out, the flares were on and you were stuck in the back because Dad couldn't face getting a car with four doors, it was the business.

FIAT X1/9

PRODUCTION: 1972–89
0–60MPH: 12 seconds
TOP SPEED: 100mph
CRISIS RATING: 1

One car that's seldom on the radar for the Happy Shopper playboy is a mid-engine Italian roadster. But Fiat twigged and, never a company afraid to cut a few corners to turn a profit, developed the X1/9.

This tiny, pretty sports car had almost all the essential ingredients to ensure unparalleled success in a market where it would undercut its competition two or three times over. It was, after all, Italian, albeit the Italian equivalent of Rover. The engine was mounted in the middle, even though it was only 75bhp and jammed into a space so small it ought only to be used for stashing your change. And the roof came off, although if it hadn't, 50 per cent of buyers wouldn't have been able to get inside.

There's no doubt that the X1/9 handled well, but it was infamous for getting severely feisty in the wet. It was also so aggressively keen on rusting at the slightest provocation that the structural integrity of the steering rack was occasionally compromised. Not a car for the faint-hearted, then. Nor anyone above average height.

MG MIDGET

PRODUCTION: 1961–79
0–60MPH: 20 seconds
TOP SPEED: 87mph
CRISIS RATING: 5 (for the boys, Ducky)

A tidy example of the tricky sexual politics in motoring, the MG Midget was an inherently sportier alternative to the ubiquitous MGB Roadster, but no self-respecting male could go within a hundred yards of one because it made him look like a big girl. This is a shame on reflection, because when it came to quintessential English open-air motoring, you'd struggle to beat the honesty and purity of the Midget.

It still kicked around for almost twenty years, despite those sizeable moments of heterosexual self-doubt it engendered in any man who got too close. Getting progressively more modern in the process (daft stuff like windows that actually wound down!), the Midget gradually lost the very thing that made it so appealing in the first place: it was brilliantly basic.

Still, BMC shifted awfully close to a quarter of a million of the things, so there were either a lot of sporty girls out there, or a lot of men with a very deep secret.

FOUR
IMPATIENCE
AS A VIRTUE

BMW **M5**

PRODUCTION: 1985–8
0–60MPH: 6.2 seconds
TOP SPEED: 153mph
CRISIS RATING: 0

For the man who had abandoned all hope of emptying the nest in his own lifetime, whose spotty adolescent offspring remained prone across the sofas and farting into their duvets at well gone midday, hope sprang eternal. For his plight was replicated a hundred times over in the boardrooms and design studios of major motoring manufacturers across the globe. And the bigwigs felt his pain.

BMW created the first M5 to provide proper sports car performance in a conventional four-door saloon. The company's own racing technicians hand-built each one, taking a boggo 5-Series and stuffing a modified version of the engine from their M1 supercar under the bonnet. The result was not only the fastest production saloon in the world, but also the birth of a legend that lives to this day.

With 280bhp on tap, the first M5 gave a spiritual kick up the chuff to an entire generation of grumpy middle-aged men. Suddenly the commute was something to be savoured, Sunday lunch at the in-laws an agony to relish, the school run a prospect your children would regard with mortal dread. Truly, Dad was back.

FERRARI 400

PRODUCTION: 1976–89
0–60MPH: 8 seconds
TOP SPEED: 149mph
CRISIS RATING: 3

Own a Ferrari in 1966, and like it or not you'd have a house full of kids in ten years time. You were that irresistible. Now Ferrari obviously felt some sense of responsibility for recklessly terminating its clientele's happy bachelorhood, because in 1976 it launched the 400. This was the dullest product ever to sport the prancing horse, a slab-sided, boxy four-seater with a shortage of power and, for the first time ever on a Ferrari, an automatic gearbox. This tragedy of a transmission was a meagre three-speed unit bought from General Motors of all people, perfectly suited to sapping the last vestiges of sporting pretension from that underperforming 4.8-litre V12.

But it didn't matter then, and it doesn't really matter now either. It's a Ferrari for God's sake, a bona fide (well, nearly) Italian thoroughbred that you can put the wife and two lanky kids in. A blinding light on the tarmac road to Damascus. Well, almost.

MITSUBISHI LANCER TURBO

PRODUCTION: 1981–3
0–60MPH: 7.1 seconds
TOP SPEED: 125mph
CRISIS RATING: 0

The major problem with kids, aside from cocking up your sports car-owning destiny, is that they're expensive little buggers. They need shoes, clothes, nit combs and all that. Nevertheless, the adoption agencies went rather quiet in 1983, a bizarre social phenomenon that anthropologists have only just attributed to Mitsubishi and its Lancer EX 2000 Turbo.

At last, here was a cheap, sensible-looking four-door saloon with a big boot and enough poke to terrify your squawking brood into white-knuckled silence for the duration of any journey. It was also reliable by any standards, let alone those of a normal sports car, and economical enough that you needn't spend more money driving to work than you earned while you were there. A modern revelation.

Of course nowadays the Lancer is the cop-baiter's car de jour, but back then it was a sleeper: understated, under the radar, but seriously quick. The turbo eked 168bhp from its 2.0-litre engine, meaning it could hit its 125mph top speed in less than 16 seconds.

And the beauty of it all was that the wife wouldn't have clue until you dropped a cog on the way back from Grandma's and she nearly swallowed her tongue.

CITROËN SM

PRODUCTION: 1970–4
0–60MPH: 8.2 seconds
TOP SPEED: 141mph
CRISIS RATING: 4

The French will always do things differently. By which we generally mean make a total balls-up. And yet you can't help but look back with a certain fondness, even admiration, on the fruits of their wine-soaked labours.

Perhaps the most ridiculous thing they ever did was the Citroën SM, a sort of national midlife crisis in car form. One particularly boozy afternoon in Citroën HQ, someone convinced the man with the cheque book to buy a Maserati and nick its engines.

So it was that in 1970 a coupé based on the DS saloon appeared with a 2.7-litre V6 Maserati engine sending 170bhp through the front wheels. You could hear a pin drop from Paris to Peking. Never had anything sounded so weird on paper, or looked it in the metal.

In actual fact, the SM was incredible. It rode like you had a head full of Valium, but still handled sweetly thanks to a radical new type of power steering. It also had ground-breaking ideas like headlights that turned in conjunction with the steering wheel. But no one bought it except for Ugandan dictator Idi Amin, who is rumoured to have had seven. And with an endorsement like that, Citroën went bust in 1974.

AUDI **RS2**

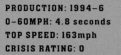

PRODUCTION: 1994–6
0–60MPH: 4.8 seconds
TOP SPEED: 163mph
CRISIS RATING: 0

Not every petrolhead of yesteryear was clinging desperately to his singleton status. In fact, back in the mid-'90s, Europe echoed to the sound of straining bedsprings as a whole generation was spawned solely to justify the purchase of an Audi RS2.

An experimental project between Audi and Porsche, the former took the fastest, four-wheel drive version of its workaday 80 Avant, and let Porsche do very dirty things to it. The result was essentially an axe-wielding madman dressed by Marks & Spencer, a 300bhp turbo-charged estate car capable of hitting 60mph in 4.8 seconds and only topping out at 163mph because Audi realized enough was enough.

Porsche also re-did all the suspension and braking, meaning the RS2 cornered and stopped like the best of the high-performance sports cars of its day and beyond.

A sublime and infallible reason to pop the question, the RS2 was Cupid with an intercooler.

LAMBORGHINI **ESPADA**

PRODUCTION: 1968–78
0–60MPH: 5.9 seconds
TOP SPEED: 152mph
CRISIS RATING: 4

True exotica should not be denied our most fertile types, but all too seldom in automotive history have the sounds of howling V12 and shrieking child overlapped on an empty stretch of autostrada. Sure, there have been a few 2+2 configurations that fitted the brief, but only in your offspring's infancy. The Lamborghini Espada remains the one true supercar that was big enough to cosset a full-sized family and all their clobber and still make you look like a lottery winner in a hurry to get naked.

Considering its scarcity today, it's hard to believe that the Espada was in production for a decade and actually out-sold the iconic Miura in the process. With impossibly impractical proportions and the sort of styling that would age even faster than its driver, the Espada was always destined for the Also-Ran Hall of Infamy. But bear in mind that you can pick one up now for the price of a Ford Focus and, well, there's a row brewing with the wife already…

LOTUS **SEVEN**

PRODUCTION: 1970–3
0–60MPH: 4.5 seconds
TOP SPEED: 130mph
CRISIS RATING: 3

What, you might well ask, is a Lotus Seven doing in a chapter dedicated to the more practical means of dealing with your own mortality? No four-door super saloon here! Good grief, you don't even get one door, let alone a boot. But the DIY DNA of the Seven actually makes it the optimum choice for the savvier dad for a number of reasons.

First up, you have to keep the family car, so no hideous tangles with your other half. Secondly, it's cheap enough in nut-and-bolt form to make two cars a realistic proposition, so no toe-curling chats with your bank manager required. And thirdly, it's so breathtakingly complicated and badly machined that you will spend every minute of free time for the next two years stuck in your garage trying to build it, thereby eliminating any trace of family life from your youthful, high-octane existence.

Only produced for three years in the 1970s, the outrageously ugly Series IV Seven was perhaps the greatest motoring proponent of the 'If it ain't broke...' adage. Boxy fibreglass bodywork replaced minimal aluminium curves, the car getting bigger, heavier and slower. With sales on the skids Lotus flogged the Seven to Caterham, who went back to basics and have traded on the midlife crisis ever since.

MASERATI QUATTROPORTE

PRODUCTION: 1994–2000
0–60MPH: Maybe
TOP SPEED: See above
CRISIS RATING: 4

Now the original Quattroporte was a beautiful-looking thing, and today's offering has a place in all but the hardest of hearts, but Maserati's designers did have the odd off-day. Or, as it transpired, the odd off-couple of-decades.

Things went from really very bad to truly unbelievably worse from about the mid-1970s to the mid-'90s, when a man called Marcello Gandini came along. He was the guy responsible for nothing less than the Lamborghini Countach, so Maser's money should've been pretty safe with Marcello. Not quite.

He penned this slap-in-the-face of a car in 1994, including, as if it were something to shout about, his 'trademark' angular rear wheel arch.

Powered by a 2.8-litre bi-turbo V6 that had as little chance of working in the factory as it did on your drive, the Quattroporte had all the things that were wrong with Italian sports cars and none of the things that were right. To wit, it didn't work moving or standing still.

Ferrari bought out Maserati four years later and began a ruthless regime of improving production standards. The Quattroporte lasted two more years, but even the prancing horse couldn't flog a dead one.

FIVE
UNDERTAKING THE JONESES

MERCEDES 450 SLC

PRODUCTION: 1973–81
0–60MPH: 9.0 seconds
TOP SPEED: 136mph
CRISIS RATING: 3

The challenges facing middle-aged man are myriad and complex. Denial of one's decline into decrepitude is an obvious must, but there are subtler social necessities for the enfeebled of follicle and meaty of midriff. In some walks of life, for example, it's far more important to appear quietly successful than brazenly rolling in it. And this is where cars such as the Mercedes SLC make their mark.

Based on the sort of posh saloon that would've got your neighbours' curtains twitching anyway, it discreetly dials in a dose of youthful vigour by dispensing with rear doors or a B-pillar. So you still end up with a Mercedes (seal of approval from the ladies who lunch) but you also get a coupé (guaranteed semblance of virility).

Perhaps the greatest attribute of the SLC, however, is the fact that despite those missing rear doors, it still has proper rear seats. This means you can shoehorn your rug rat inside and no one will be able to tell you've even got one. A sort of smoke-and-mirrors alternative to the elixir of eternal youth. Genius.

JAGUAR XJ-S

PRODUCTION: 1976–96
0–60MPH: 6.5 seconds
TOP SPEED: 157mph
CRISIS RATING: 4

The simplest way of expressing your toupee-related anguish is to buy a car that couldn't be better suited to the old and infirm if it were a hearse. The Jaguar XJ-S stinks of mothballs and mildew, Granny's perfume and stale cigar smoke, and that's before it's even left the factory.

Designed to replace the iconic E-Type, the XJ-S first appeared in 1976, fitted with a 5.3-litre V12 engine. Despite being one of the few cars outside of Italian exotica with such an engine, and regardless of the reasonable straight-line performance that it provided, the XJ-S was always a long way from being a sports car. Almost every one sold used an automatic gearbox, and the styling did precious little for a generation brought up on the rakish E-Type.

Nevertheless, Jaguar persevered, making the XJ-S for some twenty years in both coupé and convertible form. It survived an oil crisis, various attempts at racing, dubious unofficial convertible efforts and even an estate version. Engine reliability remained a problem throughout much of its life though, and rust took hold like a rash from the Grim Reaper.

PORSCHE 924

PRODUCTION: 1976–88
0–60MPH: 10.1 seconds
TOP SPEED: 125mph
CRISIS RATING: 2

In the late 1970s a car appeared that seemed to offer everything the frustrated family man could desire. It was affordable, sporty, practical, spacious, and had a badge on the bonnet that snapped knicker elastic at a thousand yards. Except there was a catch. It turns out it wasn't affordable, sporty, practical or spacious, and despite having a Porsche badge on the front, everyone knew that under the bonnet it had an Audi engine which had been stolen from a truck.

An ignominious start to life for the 924 then, especially since it was actually rather good. Porsche had designed it for Volkswagen to sell as a cost-effective sports car, and it did a fine job, giving it near-perfect balance, great looks (back then) and tough, simple mechanicals. But the bean counters at VW got cold feet after the 1973 oil crisis and sold the whole project back to Porsche at a bargain price.

Having a water-cooled engine upfront spawned a new design direction for Porsche that survived right into the mid-1990s and actually made enough money at a shaky time to keep the company afloat. Against the odds the 924 ran and ran, but the pricey, prang-prone 911 was, and still is, the Porker of choice for the man in meltdown.

MASERATI BI-TURBO SPYDER

PRODUCTION: 1984–91
0-60MPH: 6.7 seconds
TOP SPEED: 134mph
CRISIS RATING: 4

One surefire way to send a shiver of collective envy through the suburbs was to buy a convertible. And better yet, an Italian one. After all, no one else round there would have racing pedigree, two whole turbos and a cockpit slathered in enough cured cow to give McDonald's the moral high ground. What could possibly go wrong?

More than anyone could ever have imagined, as it turned out. The early 1980s was a period of production at Maserati that not just the Italians, but mankind as a whole, would do well to draw a thick veil over. These cars seldom made it from factory to forecourt without near terminal engine problems, due both to their small capacity, high-stress design and Maserati's own legendarily crap build protocol.

Watched by smirking neighbours from behind crocheted curtains, the walk to the train station could scarcely seem longer.

BMW 8 SERIES

PRODUCTION: 1989–99
0–60MPH: 7.1 seconds
TOP SPEED: 155mph
CRISIS RATING: 4

A recurrent theme in car design for 40-somethings, one that reflects the increasing dilapidation of the core demographic, is creature comforts. You get old, you get creaky, and you get used to certain luxuries. So when the time comes to buy something a little sporty, be damned if you're going to give it all up.

BMW's 8 Series is a car that simply screams 'Fat Bastard'; its scale, opulence and complexity all utterly at odds with the company's sporting ambitions. Costing around 1.5 billion Deutschmarks to develop, and that's in mid 1980s money, the 8 Series debuted radical technology like the drive-by-wire throttle, multi-link rear axle and ultra-aerodynamic bodywork designed by computers. Every conceivable onboard gimmick also meant that it was hopelessly heavy, hideously expensive to run and prone to go wrong.

Even today, seeing an 8 Series drive past at speed is not unlike watching a dangerously overweight stockbroker lumber around a squash court en route to a massive coronary.

BENTLEY **TURBO R**

PRODUCTION: 1985—92
0—60MPH: 6.7 seconds
TOP SPEED: 152mph
CRISIS RATING: 1

Until there are ice cubes in Hell's tea, no self-respecting Bentley owner is going to buy a sports car. But that doesn't mean he can't have a rather refined sort of midlife crisis, dignity largely still intact, by splashing out on something with a little bit more poke. The Turbo R was Bentley's answer to the question nobody had bothered to ask. In essence, it was just a way of making a car that was even more expensive than the one it was already only selling to sheikhs and plutocrats.

A 6.75-litre Rolls Royce V8 ensured that all Bentleys could shift, but adding a turbocharger doubled available power for the R, while stiffening up the suspension, and giving it light alloy wheels meant it could, in theory, now handle as well. If, however, throwing around a 2.4 tonne turbo-charged humidor was your idea of fun, you had bigger things to worry about than getting old.

BAUR TC

PRODUCTION: 1978–85
0–60MPH: 8.3 seconds
TOP SPEED: 135mph
CRISIS RATING: 2

Back in the late 1970s, the BMW 3 Series was establishing itself across Europe and the USA as the runaround de jour for the wealthier sophisticate. But from Miami to Monte Carlo something vital was missing for our middle-aged motorist: there was no lengthy exposure to UV rays. You see, the mechanically-minded purists back in Germany didn't really give a lot of thought to a soft-top. Not really their scene.

Enter Karosserie Baur, a local coachwork outfit that had been chopping up BMWs since before the war. With the blessing of the big cheeses, Baur designed and built a sort of targa-cum-cabriolet roof for the 3 Series that was really neither one thing nor the other. But it did mean you could get burnt while driving or stand up on the backseat at the beach, an invaluable attribute ably demonstrated here.

Despite making the 3 Series wobbly and weird-looking, the Baur TC (that's Top Convertible, obviously) was a massive success and BMW realized the male menopause was a huge money-spinner. But even when it brought out a proper 3 Series convertible of its own, people still wanted Baur's hacksaw job. There's just no accounting for hormones.

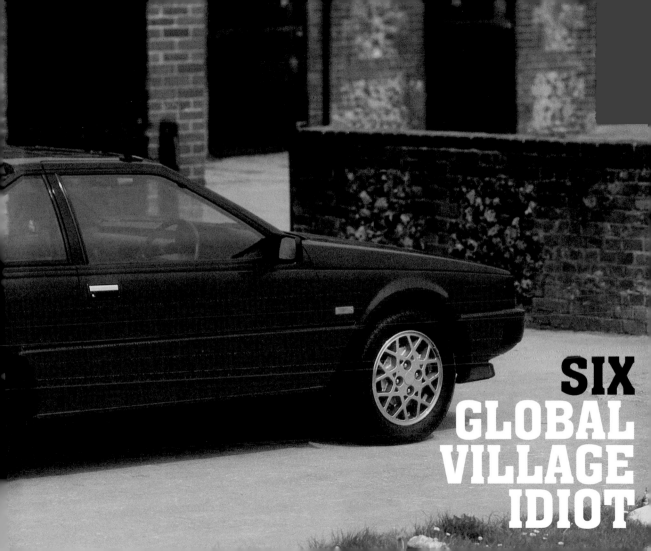

SIX
GLOBAL
VILLAGE
IDIOT

SAAB **SONETT**

PRODUCTION: 1960–74
0–60MPH: 12.5 seconds
TOP SPEED: 93mph
CRISIS RATING: 3

It's tempting to regard the motoring manifestation of middle-age spread as a localized problem, something we only see in our husbands and dads, but there's no getting away from the terrible truth: the affliction is global.

Even a country as straight-laced as Sweden, the land responsible for the most sensible car in history with the Volvo estate, has had its moments. In 1960 Saab set about making a fibreglass two-stroke two-seater. It produced 60bhp, meaning its driver would visibly age on the way to 60mph and be collecting his pension by the time top speed was reached. The Sonett looked ridiculous from every angle, and when people found out it was front-wheel drive and that the pop-up lights had to be raised manually, the game was up.

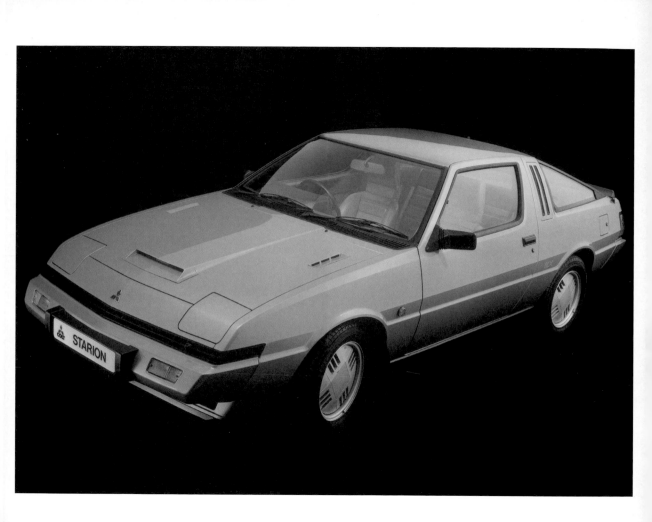

MITSUBISHI **STARION**

PRODUCTION: 1982–90
0–60MPH: 7.8 seconds
TOP SPEED: 129mph
CRISIS RATING: 2

Japan had a lot to answer for when it came to producing half-arsed sports cars. It also made the whole thing worse by giving them spectacularly stupid names. Legend has it that Mitsubishi wanted to call their latest turbo-charged sports car the Stallion, but there were some issues with pronunciation during a vital long-distance phone call.

Nevertheless, the Starion went on to be a significant milestone for Mitsubishi and Japanese cars in general, ushering in the era of turbo-charging and attaining remarkable success in world motor sport due to its unprecedented reliability.

The only hang-up was that everyone thought it looked bloody awful and suspected the name might be some sort of xenophobic joke, so it sold badly and was eventually abandoned.

CORVETTE CONVERTIBLE

PRODUCTION: 1953–present
0–60MPH: 5.6 seconds (1986)
TOP SPEED: 124mph (1986)
CRISIS RATING: 4

Americans obsess about being self-made men. It's that whole 'Land of the Free' thing where you can buy a hotdog cart aged 16, and ten years later you're a tax-dodging billionaire with a mansion and a Mexican manservant. So there's no car that piqued the pride of our unloved cousins back in the 1980s quite like the Corvette convertible. It was a blue-collar dream: the epitome of triumph over adversity, the jewel in the capitalist crown. A piece of under-engineered plastic shite.

The thing about the Corvette that no American would admit, probably because they genuinely didn't notice, is that it was utterly dreadful. It had an enormous agricultural engine barely connected to a wobbly fibreglass body, an interior finish the Malaysian car industry would baulk at, and cornering ability more commonly associated with super tankers. Small wonder the 'Vette was affordable to all. It wasn't worth anything.

Still, that didn't put anyone off, and Chevrolet's tacky two-seater has now been in production for well over fifty years, a full half-century of bald spots and beer bellies.

LANCIA BETA MONTECARLO

PRODUCTION: 1975–81
0–60MPH: 10 seconds
TOP SPEED: 112mph
CRISIS RATING: 3

If ever alarm bells should have gone off across Italy, it was when the Fiat X1/9's big brother appeared. Badged up as a Lancia, however, it managed to slip under the radar and went to market in 1975.

It took a whole three years before they were recalled because the over-eager front brakes were causing cars to lock up if they so much as sniffed the scent of rain. Production was halted, the servos removed, and, after a fashion, the problem solved.

True to cut-price Italian form, the Beta Montecarlo looked fantastic but was woefully short on grunt. It was also unreliable and likely to rust if it was raining on the other side of the world. The rear chassis cross member was made perilously thin to save weight and cost, and when this rotted through the car could effectively collapse. This meant that not only did precious few people buy one back then, but that incredibly almost none are still kicking around today.

MAZDA RX-7

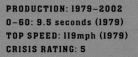

PRODUCTION: 1979–2002
0–60: 9.5 seconds (1979)
TOP SPEED: 119mph (1979)
CRISIS RATING: 5

While most European manufacturers were sticking to what they knew, the 1980s was a time of radical invention in Japan — some of it with bizarre consequences. Mazda launched the rotary-engined RX-7 in 1979, creating a peculiar quandary for both phallocentric men and their Freudian critics. Here was a sports car with a tiny engine. Was it still manly? To make matters worse, the engine was named after the German bloke who pioneered the idea almost 30 years before — and he was called Wankel. Confusion was rife.

As it happened, the Wankel rotary engine was ingenious, being lightweight, reliable and very smooth. But it was also exceptionally thirsty, and wolfing down the petrol at a time when oil and money were in short supply did even more damage to the RX-7 than its uncertain position as a proper penis extension.

The car was dropped in 1984, but Mazda periodically had another Wankel, reinventing the RX-7 twice more by 1992, and rumour has it they may be at it again right now.

RENAULT ALPINE A310

PRODUCTION: 1976–84
0–60MPH: 8.1 seconds
TOP SPEED: 131mph
CRISIS RATING: 1

The French car industry was nothing if not ambitious. Amidst the chaos of the 1973 oil crisis, Renault saw a hole in the market for a home-grown alternative to the Porsche 911. So they bailed out the cash-strapped Alpine sports car company and promptly began selling the Alpine A310 as a fully-fledged Renault to all those Gallic patriots with a need for obscure, locally-built, fibreglass, rear-engined sports cars.

Sadly there weren't quite as many of them as Renault had hoped and the A310 never got the attention it deserved at home or abroad. In its eight-year production run, just over 9,000 A310s were made; big numbers for Alpine but a drop in the ocean for Renault.

The A310 went like stink and handled remarkably well for a French car with an engine hanging off the back axle, but its legacy is little more than a blip on the automotive timeline.

BITTER SC

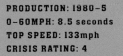

PRODUCTION: 1980–5
0–60MPH: 8.5 seconds
TOP SPEED: 133mph
CRISIS RATING: 4

Even the ever-sensible and ruthlessly competent Germans have the odd dirty secret in the annals of automobilia. And the Bitter SC is positively filthy. Based on the already pretty horrendous Vauxhall Senator, the Bitter was launched in 1980 as a coupé, to be followed four years later by a convertible. Bitter actually had a great reputation at this stage with its CD coupé, and was looking to grow its market share with a modern, high-quality and luxurious four-seater.

In a gamble of comedic proportions, Bitter out-sourced the fabrication of the SC's bodywork to an unproven Italian company, and within months the first customer cars had begun to rust. The contract was quickly withdrawn and the SC built by a more reputable outfit.

In the end the SC was well-made and expensively finished, but this didn't balance out the fact that it looked like a Ferrari 400 drawn by a five-year-old and everyone knew it had a Vauxhall engine. Compounding Bitter's problems was a woefully slow production rate of between one and two cars a week. This meant that by 1985 the coffers were empty and work stopped for good.

DATSUN 240-Z

PRODUCTION: 1969–78
0–60MPH: 8.2 seconds
TOP SPEED: 109mph
CRISIS RATING: 1

Not every sports car that came out of Japan in the 1970s and '80s was a total humiliation for the over-ripe type who queued up to capitalize on their affordability and build quality. Some have even gone on to be desirable classics. Well, one.

The Datsun 240-Z first appeared in 1969, consciously designed and styled to take the American muscle car on at its own game.

Growing in engine size and luxury throughout the '70s, it firmly established itself as a sporting icon. It looked the part, was seriously rapid for its day and, crucially in the performance market, just didn't go wrong.

The fact that the Yanks gave the 240-Z their seal of approval, buying over 30,000 in its first full year of export, did huge things for the credibility of Japanese sports cars, and a fair bit for international relations.

FERRARI 308 GTS

PRODUCTION: 1975-85
0-60MPH: 6.5 seconds
TOP SPEED: 159mph
CRISIS RATING: 5

No round-up of international ignominy would be complete without a Ferrari. Replace high living and Italian escort with high rise and Escort XR3i, and suddenly there's nothing quite so desperate as owning a 308.

This is the era of 3,000-mile engine rebuilds and servicing costs that could feed a family of four for a year. This was also the period when Ferrari started to reach a wider audience, and before long every crook and Cheshire businessman was kicking the last vestiges of life out of his GTS as it steamed contentedly on the hard shoulder.

The significance of the 308 shouldn't be understated, and nor can it be denied that this is still a seriously beautiful and desirable thing, but any car that spent the best part of a decade being driven round Hawaii by Tom Selleck in a floral shirt and a pair of denim hot pants had already lost its edge.

DELOREAN DMC-12

PRODUCTION: 1981–2
0–60MPH: 8.5 seconds
TOP SPEED: 130mph
CRISIS RATING: 5

What do you get if you cross Northern Ireland with an American drug dealer? Not a massive arms cache for the IRA, oddly, but the DeLorean DMC-12. This extraordinary-looking thing is the product of one man's personal midlife crisis, when he invested a fortune in building an impossibly bad sports car in a poor suburb of Belfast.

The DeLorean was a classic case of a sweet dream turned sour, with its stunning prototype proving both financially unsound and mechanically unsuited for mass production.

Regardless of this, the factory opened at the start of 1981, was quickly filled with totally inexperienced Irish labourers, and within a year was in receivership. It had managed to churn out an impressive 9,000 cars in that time, all of them beset by basic quality and design flaws that left their owners seething and stranded.

John DeLorean, seeing the writing on the wall, had got himself embroiled in a farcically complicated money-laundering scam that involved lorry-loads of cocaine and undercover feds. He was promptly nicked and eventually cleared on the grounds of entrapment, but by then it was all over for John and his DMC-12.

MITSUBISHI SAPPORO

PRODUCTION: 1976–83
0–60MPH: 10.5 seconds
TOP SPEED: 110mph
CRISIS RATING: 3

Machiavellian marketing types rely upon convincing us that we absolutely have to have something that five minutes ago we didn't even want, let alone need. This is particularly effective when they combine new cars with old men, and probably the only reason the Mitsubishi Sapporo ever existed.

The company already had a coupé, crappy though it was, so decided to spin the Sapporo as 'a personal luxury car'. In translation, that means it was small, but chock-full of gimmicks: perfect for the overpaid and undersexed.

Essentially just a cut-down saloon car, the Sapporo was even sold with diesel engines, which in the late 1970s was about as far removed from luxury as you could humanly get. But the novelty of things like an integrated aerial, a state-of-the-art stereo and power everything proved that, when it comes to cars, you *can* happily polish a turd.

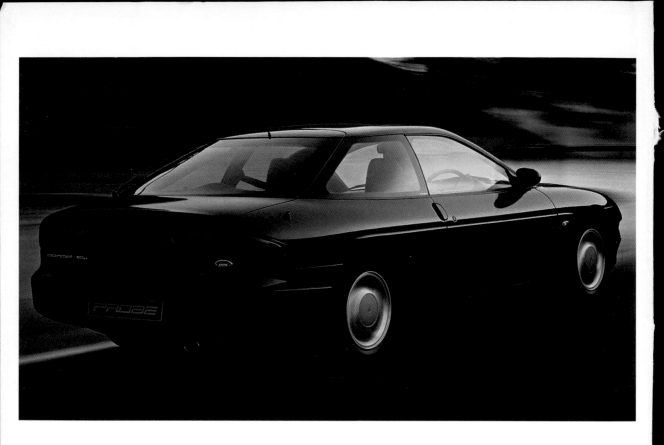

FORD PROBE

PRODUCTION: 1989–97
0–60MPH: 8.5 seconds
TOP SPEED: 140mph
CRISIS RATING: 5

Having circumnavigated the globe smirking at Johnny Foreigner's tat, it's only right that we finish on Britain's most risible excuse for a sports car. When Ford killed off the Capri there was a gap in the market for another affordable, desirable, blue-collar coupé. Ford took no notice of this, however, and made the Probe instead.

With its sleek, futuristic styling the name Probe was meant to conjure up images of pioneering and conquest, but inevitably it just made people think of visiting the sexual health clinic. It was also basically just a Mazda underneath, front-wheel drive, slow and way too expensive.

In no time, the Probe was associated with deluded sales reps and frustrated middle-management. The only saving grace here is that the rest of the British car-buying public spoke with its feet when it came to the Probe, and waited for the bus. After eight years Ford had sold just over 800,000 units. It was time to pull the plug.

1 2 3 4 5 6 7 8 9 10

Published in 2008 by BBC Books,
an imprint of Ebury Publishing.
A Random House Group Company

The Random House Group Limited
Reg. No. 954009

Addresses for companies within the
Random House Group can be found at
www.randomhouse.co.uk

A CIP catalogue record for this book is
available from the British Library.

ISBN 978 1 846 07497 4

The Random House Group Limited
makes every effort to ensure that the
papers used in our books are made from
trees that have been legally sourced
from well-managed and credibly certified
forests. Our paper procurement policy
can be found on www.randomhouse.co.uk

Commissioning editor: Lorna Russell
Designer: Smith & Gilmour
Illustrator: Rude
Production controller: Antony Heller

Colour origination by Altaimage
Printed and bound in Singapore by
Tien Wah Press

Picture Credits

BBC Books would like to thank the
following for providing photographs.
While every effort has been made to
trace copyright holders, we would like
to apologize should there be any
errors or omissions.

Lotus Seven Register: p83

All other photographs are reproduced
from original sales brochures stocked
by Pooks Motor Books of Rothley,
Leicestershire (Tel: 0116 237 6222;
email: pooks.motorbooks@virgin.net).